2013

Poems Inspired by Channelled Information

J K ROBERTS

BALBOA.
PRESS

A DIVISION OF HAY HOUSE

WRITTEN AND ILLUSTRATED
BY J K ROBERTS
kateartspeak@hotmail.com

Balboa Press books may be ordered through booksellers or by contacting:

Balboa Press
A Division of Hay House
1663 Liberty Drive
Bloomington, IN 47403
www.balboapress.com.au
1-(877) 407-4847

ISBN: 978-1-4525-0956-3 (sc)
ISBN: 978-1-4525-0957-0 (e)

Because of the dynamic nature of the Internet, any web addresses or links contained in this book may have changed since publication and may no longer be valid. The views expressed in this work are solely those of the author and do not necessarily reflect the views of the publisher, and the publisher hereby disclaims any responsibility for them.

The author of this book does not dispense medical advice or prescribe the use of any technique as a form of treatment for physical, emotional, or medical problems without the advice of a physician, either directly or indirectly. The intent of the author is only to offer information of a general nature to help you in your quest for emotional and spiritual well-being. In the event you use any of the information in this book for yourself, which is your constitutional right, the author and the publisher assume no responsibility for your actions.

Any people depicted in stock imagery provided by Thinkstock are models, and such images are being used for illustrative purposes only.
Certain stock imagery © Thinkstock.

Printed in the United States of America

Balboa Press rev. date: 06/06/2013

CONTENTS

PROLOGUE

TWENTY THIRTEEN IS SPECIAL YEAR OF CELEBRATION
MARKING OFFICIAL BEGINNING OF OUR NEW ERA
ABOUT MIDWAY POINT IN A THIRTY YEAR TURN-AROUND
EVERYONE ON THE PLANET
COMES NEARER AND DEARER
FOR WE HAVE
THANKFULLY
REACHED THE POINT OF NO RETURN
TO PAST STRUGGLES AND MISERIES ON OUR PLANET EARTH
THE GRAND PLANETARY ALIGNMENT HAS NOW OCCURRED
DIVINE ALIGNMENT IS ASSURED
THIS IS OUR REBIRTH

TWENTY THIRTEEN

THINK OF THE YEAR TWENTY THIRTEEN
AS A BRIGHT ISLAND OUT OF TIME
AS A GIFT FROM THE UNIVERSE
TO HELP HUMANS REACH THE SUBLIME
HOW WILL YOU USE THIS GIFT DIVINE

LOOPHOLE

THE PAST IS GONE
LET THE GOOD TIMES ROLL
HAVE WE BEEN CAUGHT IN MELODRAMA
NOW KNOW
EMOTIONS WE CAN CONTROL
DID WE EXPECT TO REPEAT TRAUMA
AD NAUSEAM
THAT IS A SAD GOAL
DID WE THINK WAR WAS EVERLASTING
THOUGH THERE IS NO CONFLICT IN THE SOUL
LET US STOP OLD CARPING AND GRASPING
LET'S FIND
AND USE
THE DIVINE LOOPHOLE

YEAR OF THE SNAKE

TWENTY THIRTEEN IS THE YEAR OF THE SNAKE
AND THE SNAKE HAS ALWAYS BEEN WIDE AWAKE
NOTICE KEEN SNAKE EYES
THEY ARE NOT BLINKING
SOMETIMES THEY PRETEND THERE IS HOODWINKING
WHEN KUNDALINI SEEMS TO BE SLEEPING
THE GODS AND THE ANGELS ARE NOT WEEPING
CONSCIOUSNESS KNOWS IT'S A TIME OF WAITING
NOW THE HULLABALOO IS ABATING
THE SNAKE IS CALLING FOR DRAMATIC CHANGE
WHAT IN YOU LIFE WILL YOU NOW REARRANGE
IN THIS YEAR OF THE CARING WATER SNAKE
TRANSFORMATION IS HERE
WE CANNOT FAKE
DISPLAYING ALL COLOURS OF THE RAINBOW
THE WHOLE WORLD HAS NEW CREDO
AND NEW HALO

OPEN ARMS

1N TWENTY TWELVE
OUR EARTH CAME THROUGH
GRAND ALIGNMENT
FROM THE CENTRAL SUN
OF THE UNIVERSE
SALAAMS
CITIZENS OF EARTH
READY FOR NEW ASSIGNMENT
LET TWENTY THIRTEEN WELCOME YOU
WITH OPEN ARMS
YOU WILL KNOW
IF YOU HAVE LOWERED ALL DEFENCES
YOU'LL BE FREE
IF YOU HAVE LAID DOWN ALL WEAPONRY
YOU CAN RESPOND
IF YOU'VE GIVEN UP ALL PRETENCES

MORE LOVE

IN TWENTY THIRTEEN
LOVELIGHT
EXCEEDS ALL CHARTS
WHEN WE FIND MORE LOVE
BLOSSOMING IN OUR HEARTS
WE'RE READY TO USE
THE CELESTIAL ARTS
THEN
THE SAME OLD PATHWAYS
WILL FIND NEW ENDINGS
THEY MAY HAVE NEW BEGINNINGS
AND NEW TURNINGS
WHAT HAPPENS
IF WE LOSE SAD REMEMBERINGS
LET US ENJOY
UNEXPECTED
NEW
YEARNINGS

WINDS OF CHANGE STILL BLOWING

TWENTY TWELVE
DRAGON OPENS THE DOOR
TWENTY THIRTEEN
WE KNOW THERE IS MORE
SNAKE'S TRANSFORMATION
READY TO SOAR
HUMANKIND
SHALL WE ALL BE IN AWE

WINDS OF CHANGE
STILL BLOWING
FAST AND TRUE
OUT OF THE STEW
INTO THE WIDE BLUE
LET WIND BLOW YOUR MIND
BECOME THE NEW YOU

SECRETS

WE ON EARTH HAVE COME THROUGH SO VERY MUCH
WE EXPLORE
WE LEARN
WE DO NOT LOSE TOUCH
OUR SOULS
STILL AS WHITE AND FREE AS EGRETS
TWENTY THIRTEEN HAS ITS WONDROUS SECRETS
WAITING TO UNFOLD WHEN THE TIME IS RIPE
HAVE THE SECRETS BEEN HIDDEN IN PLAIN SIGHT
DARE SCHISM
CHASM
CAN'T FALL OVER EDGE
1S TWENTY THIRTEEN THE SUSPENSION BRIDGE
ACROSS OUR HUMAN GAP OF UNKNOWING
THROUGH OUR TRIALS OUR COURAGE HAS BEEN GROWING
NOW WE LET GO ALL FEAR OF THE UNKNOWN
EAGER TO UNDERSTAND HOW WIND HAS BLOWN
HELPING US CROSS OVER TO FREEDOM'S SIDE
WHEN HEART IS PURE BRIDGE IS OPEN AND WIDE
DON'T KEEP YOURSELF IN SUSPENSE ANY MORE
LET YOUR THIRD EYE SEE CLEARLY THROUGH THE DOOR
RELAX
SIGH
DON'T CRY
LET GO CONFUSION
SEPARATION WAS
AFTER ALL
ILLUSION

TRANSITIONAL REALITY

RELAX
BREATHE DEEPLY
SIGH
LET YOURSELF FEEL THE NEW ENERGY
ARE WE NOW STEPPING INTO TRANSITIONAL REALITY
WITH IMPETUS FROM SNAKE'S METAMORPHIC FLEXIBILITY
IN PREPARATION FOR MULTIDIMENSIONAL CLARITY
EACH KNOWING OUR OWN MIND AND HEART
THERE'S NO REAL DISPARITY
ON EARTH TODAY
WE'RE GAINING COMPASSION WITH ALACRITY
WHY NOT FLIRT WITH *UNCONVENTIONAL* MATERIALITY

NO LONGER BOXED IN

WILL WE NOTICE
WHEN THE OLD WALLS ARE NOT THERE ANY MORE
WHEN WILL WE REALIZE
WE CAN SEE A FAR DISTANT SHORE
WHAT IS THE TRICK OF RISING ABOVE
NEEDLESS RESTRICTION
WHEN WILL WE SIMPLY DISSOLVE
OUTRAGEOUS OBSTRUCTION

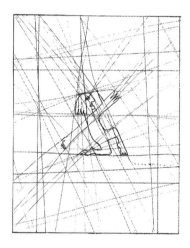

REVELATION

THE YEAR TWENTY THIRTEEN
IS A YEAR OF REVELATION
ESPECIALLY FOR THOSE WILLING TO BE
IN ELATION
ARE YOU READY TO EXPOSE YOUR HIGHEST EXPECTATION
ARE YOU ABLE TO LET YOUR HIGHER BEING TAKE CONTROL
FOR YOUR GREATEST CHANGE
WILL COME
FROM YOUR OWN
HEART
MIND
AND SOUL
FIRST OF ALL
BE AT PEACE
WITH WHAT IT MEANS
TO BE HUMAN
THEN SPEAK YOUR TRUTH
SING YOUR OWN SONG
SPONSOR
YOUR OWN EVOLUTION

CONSCIOUSNESS EVOLUTION

TOTAL FORGIVENESS
TOTAL COMPASSION
EVER-REFINING LOVE AND PERCEPTION
LIGHTING OUR WAY
INTO PURE UNITY
DO WHAT YOU LOVE
LOVE ALL THAT YOU CAN BE
RELAX
SLOW DOWN
FOLLOW YOUR TRUE FEELINGS
LEARN HOW TO TRUST YOUR INNERMOST LEANINGS
FOLLOW YOUR HEART
ON WAY TO FULFILMENT
WITH NO STRUGGLE ON WAY TO UPLIFTMENT
YOU'RE RECORDING ON A NEW HOLOGRAPH
MERGING WITH YOUR HIGHER ENLIGHTENED SELF
YOU'RE BLENDING WITH THE CORE OF YOUR BEING
ON THE WAY TO DIVINITY
ALL REACHING

FREEDOM

WE ARE GAINING THE FREEDOM TO BE FULLY HUMAN
THROUGH THE DIMENSIONS WE SHALL
DISCOVER ALL THIS MEANS
ELECTROMAGNETICALLY WE GAIN ACUMEN
WE WILL SOON BASK IN ALL THE SOLAR LIGHT WE CAN SEE
PATRIARCH HONOURS MATRIARCH AND VISA VERSA
THE FEMININE AND MASCULINE GAIN EQUALITY
EXTRATERRESTRIALS BECOME PART OF OUR PICTURE
THE PINEAL OPENS
WE RECOGNIZE ELOHIM
THE INTUITIVE AND RATIONAL WORK TOGETHER
LOWER SELF MERGES PURPOSEFULLY WITH HIGHER SELF
IN PERFECT HARMONY THEY CAN HONOUR EACH OTHER
EGO NO LONGER NEEDS KEEP US SAFE
FEAR'S A NO THING
SEE KARMA DECLINE
BOW OUT
WE NO LONGER SUFFER
AS WE CAN RE-DEFINE OUR IMMACULATE CONCEPT
TWIXT HEAVEN AND EARTH WE NO LONGER NEED A BUFFER
EAST SOUTH WEST AND NORTH
RECOGNIZE LIGHT OF INNER SUN
DENSE CARBON GIVES WAY TO CLARITY OF CRYSTALLINE
IN CLEAR LIGHT WE ARE ABLE TO SEE OURSELVES AS ONE
WITH WATER EARTH FIRE AIR AND ETHER WE SHALL REFINE
ARE OUR OWN FIVE BODIES PULSATING
FEELING FINE-SPUN
EMOTIONAL
PHYSICAL
MENTAL
SPIRITUAL
NO LONGER FORGETTING TO INCLUDE ETHEREAL
BECAUSE WE'RE NO LONGER HEMMED INTO MATERIAL
WE MANOEUVRE OUR WAY THROUGH THE ASTRAL OF 4 D
BY THE GRACE OF GOD WE GRADUATE INTO 5 D
WHERE DENSITY OF LIGHT INCREASES WHAT WE CAN BE
AND WAVES OF ILLUMINATION BRING ACTIVATION
WE KNOW WE'RE FUNCTIONING WITH DIVINE APPROBATION
BEYOND 5 D
IN THE *I AM* PRESENCE
MIRACLES WE DECREE

THIRTEEN

THIRTEEN IS OUR LUCKY NUMBER
IF WE ARE NOT AFRAID OF CHANGE
IT AWAKENS US FROM SLUMBER
IT LETS US STRETCH TIME LIKE RUBBER
IF EARTH'S READY TO REARRANGE
THIRTEEN SUGGESTS INVOCATION
THIRTEEN IS YOUR INVITATION
TO ASK FOR CHANGES YOU WISH FOR
TWENTY THIRTEEN'S AN OPEN DOOR
IT'S DARING US TO EXPECT MORE
LET OLD TIMES
OLD WAYS
UNRAVEL
MAKE NEW PLANS FOR YOUR SOUL TRAVEL
UPON A NEW WORLD
LIGHT YOUR CANDLE

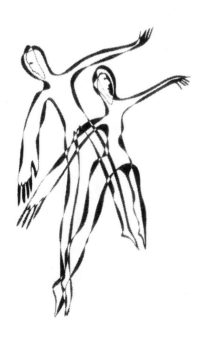

LET GO

LET GO WORRY
LET GO SORROW
LET GO STRIFE
MAGIC OF BELIEVING
CAN TRANSFORM YOUR LIFE
BE YOUR WHOLE SELF
HOLD HIGHEST ASPIRATIONS
TURN A NEW LEAF
EXPAND HIGHEST EXPECTATIONS

IT IS TIME TO HEAL

HEAR YE HUMANITY
NOW IS THE TIME TO HEAL
FOR NONE OF YOUR PAST AFFLICTIONS HAVE TO BE REAL
ON THE DOOR TO DARKNESS
WE PUT FINE BLESSINGS SEAL
SO WHEN IT OPENS ONCE AGAIN
ONLY LIGHT STREAMS FORTH
EARTH'S HUMANITY IS IN A STATE OF REBIRTH
ALL OF OUR PATHWAYS SHALL BECOME
LIGHTER HENCEFORTH
IN MULTI-DIMENSIONS WE WILL EXPAND BOARDERS
WE SHALL FIND CONCORD JOY AND PEACE IN ALL QUARTERS
GRACE
FORGIVENESS
KINDNESS
ARE THE RULING FORCES
EMERGING AND MERGING WITH TRUE LOVE UNENDING
ALL OF THE CELLS OF OUR BODIES ARE ASCENDING
SEE YOUR BODY AND YOUR WHOLE LIFE IN PURITY
DIVINE LOVE
IS THE ESSENCE OF SECURITY

SHARE

IN THE DAYS TO COME
WE'LL ONLY WISH TO SHARE OUR BLESSINGS
IN THE UNIFICATION OF THE HUMAN FAMILY
WE'LL NO LONGER BE SO ISOLATED IN OUR DWELLINGS
IN OUR STATIONS IN LIFE
OR IN OUR TOWNS AND OUR NATIONS
WE WILL RESPECT OTHER PEOPLES SPIRITUALITY
ON WHOLE PLANET
NO ONE EVER AGAIN TO BE HUNGRY
NO RIVALRY
WE'LL WORK AND PLAY TOGETHER HAPPILY
CAN YOU IMAGINE THIS ON SCALE
INTERPLANETARY

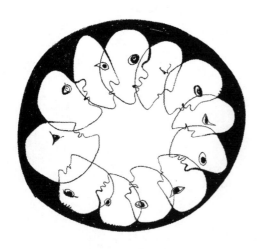

EXPLORE

HOW LONG HAVE YOU WISHED
TO EXPLORE
THE FAR AND WIDENING EXPANSIONS
OF YOUR POTENTIALITY
KNOWING THERE ARE PRIZES GALORE
HOW LONG HAVE YOU FELT LIMITED
PHYSICALLY
EMOTIONALLY
ALSO ECONOMICALLY
NOW LET'S BE UNINHIBITED
FOR WE NO LONGER HAVE TO DELVE
HANG ON TO YOUR SPATS AND YOUR HATS
IN YOUR BELFRY THERE ARE NO BATS
WE'VE PASSED SOLSTICE OF TWENTY TWELVE
TWENTY THIRTEEN IS UPON US
NOW ALL STOPS OUT
NO HOLDS ALLOWED
ALL OUR ESSAYS SHALL BE GOLD-STARRED
THE WORLD HAS CHANGED
DIDN'T YOU SUS
SURELY YOU WERE READY TO KNOW
ALL OLD BARRIERS COMING DOWN
IF YOU WISH YOU CAN PAINT THE TOWN
ALL THE COLOURS OF THE RAINBOW

INSTINCTIVE KNOWING

TO SOURCE
TO ESSENCE
MAY FAITH BE UNWAVERING
THIS IS THE SPECIAL TIME
OF OUR RE-CONNECTING
KNOW THAT THIS IS THE TIME OF OUR AWAKENING
WE ON EARTH
ARE ALL
COMING VERY MUCH CLOSER
TO PRIME ABILITY OF INSTINCTIVE KNOWING
TO THOSE IN THE KNOW
FINER INSTINCTS ARE SHOWING
AS WE BECOME LIGHTER
OUR AURAS ARE GLOWING
TO HIGHER ENERGIES WE ASK FOR EXPOSURE
TO UPLIFT US FROM OUR OUTMODED PARADIGMS
OF A BETTER FUTURE
SURELY WE SEE THE SIGNS
HOW LUCKY WE FEEL TO LIVE IN THESE CHANGING TIMES
IN THE PASSING PHASE OF BLATANT AUTHORITY
TO YOURSELF ARE YOU PAYING CLOSER ATTENTION
HIGHER STANDARDS AND VALUES HAVE OUR EXPRESSION
OF THE DIVINE IN ALL
WE HAVE COMPREHENSION
WE PROCEED WITH MORE CHARITY AND HONESTY
TAKE NOTICE
HOW MUCH MORE DO YOU ALREADY KNOW
THAN CONVENTION AGREED UPON TOO LONG AGO
DO YOU FEEL NEW ABILITIES THAT DON'T YET SHOW
ARE YOU REALIZING
THE SOURCE YOU HAVE WITHIN
THUS
ARE YOU IN TOUCH WITH HIGHER GROUP CONSCIOUSNESS
WHERE
TOWARDS ALL LIFE
PEACE AND GOODWILL ARE OBVIOUS
THANK GOD WE WILL NO LONGER BE OBLIVIOUS
AS ALL OF WORLDLY LIFE TAKES ON A HIGHER SPIN

STARS IN YOUR EYES

WHEN YOU AWAKEN IN THE MORNING
DO YOU FEEL DIVINE
DO YOU HEAR THE DAWN CHORUS
SAYING ISN'T IT SUBLIME
HAVE YOU NOTICED
YOUR LIFE IS ALREADY A MIRACLE
THOUGH YOU MAY HAVE GUESSED
YOU HAVE NOT YET SEEN THE PINNACLE
WHEN YOU SURVIVE A BAD PATCH
YOU KNOW YOU'RE UNSINKABLE
AND THINGS ARE IMPROVING
THE REVERSE IS UNTHINKABLE
YOU MAY STOP AND FEEL
WE'RE ALL GRADUALLY ASCENDING
AFTER ALL IT WILL BE EASY
TIME AND SPACE ARE BENDING
AND FOLKS WHOSE SIGHTS HAVE BEEN BENT
WILL SOON FIND *THAT* IS ENDING
WE'LL ALL COME TO REALIZE
THAT LIFE IN MORE SUBTLE REALMS
WILL BE SOFTER
EASIER
PEACE REIGNS
AND JOY OVERWHELMS
OUR VITALITY AND REALITY ARE EXPANDING
LET SPIRITS FLY HIGH ABOVE
INTO EARTH'S NEW WONDERLAND
EVEN PLANTS AND ANIMALS WILL BE FEELING
TRULY SVELTE
LOVING CARING FOR EACH OTHER
WILL BE TRULY HEARTFELT
EXPRESSIONS OF OUR DIVINITY
WILL BE NO SURPRISE
IT ISN'T ANY WONDER
THAT YOU HAVE STARS IN YOUR EYES

FLEXIBILITY

DID YOU EVER
PAINT YOURSELF INTO A CORNER
JUST SO YOU WOULD FORCE YOURSELF
TO WALK THROUGH THE WALL
OR FLY YOURSELF
BACK TO THE CENTRE OF THE ROOM
PREEN YOUR WINGS
KNOW
WITH STICKY KNEES YOU WOULD NOT CRAWL
YOU CAN ALWAYS FIND YOURSELF STUCK IN A PROBLEM
UNTIL YOU LOOSEN UP
ALLOW YOUR HEART TO SING
KNOW EVERY SITUATION HAS A SOLUTION
WHICH YOU CAN FIND
AS SOON AS YOU LET YOUR
MIND
TAKE
WING

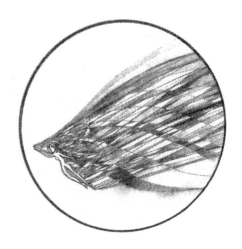

VIRTUAL REALITY

DO THOSE WHO CALL THEMSELVES REALISTS
ACCUSE YOU OF BEING A DREAMER
DO THEY SAY DON'T TELL YOURSELF STORIES
DO THEY LACK SPERO MELIORA
DO THEY LACK THE ESPRIT DE VIVA
PERHAPS THEY'RE WATCHING TOO MUCH T V
ARE THEY DRINKING TOO MUCH TEQUILA
DO THEY MISTRUST YOUR OPTIMISM
ARE THEY HELD BACK BY PRAGMATISM
WHAT IF MUCH OF WHAT THEY THINK THEY SEE
IS NOTHING MORE THAN AN ILLUSION
IT IS VIRTUAL REALITY
WHAT IF ALICE DOWN A RABBIT HOLE
KNEW GREATER REALITY THAN THEY
WHEN SCIENCE DISCOVERED THE WORMHOLE
REALITY TURNED DIFFERENT WAY
MIGHT A REALIST DIG LIKE A MOLE
HOPING HE COULD STILL
HAVE THE LAST SAY
REALIST'S HARD WORLD HATES CONFUSION
YOURS OPEN TO FLEXIBILITY
THOUGH THEY THINK YOU HAVE BEEN A SCHEMER
DABBLING IN DREAMS GAMES PLAYS AND NOVELS
WHICH FACTUAL THINK TO BE FOOLISH
YOU MAY BE MORE ACTUAL THAN THEY
WHEN SOUL MEMORY BEGINS TO FLASH
WHEN TRUE LOVE RULES
AND FALSE BECOMES FEY
YOU ARE NO LONGER HURT BY TONGUE LASH
TRUE LIFE
BECOMES
A DIFFERENT STORY

UNITY CONSCIOUSNESS

FEEL HUMANITY CHANGING
CHANGING FROM DEEP WITHIN
IN MINDS AND HEARTS
TRUER FEELINGS
KINDLY
GENUINE
IN THE MATURITY OF INCREASING PURITY
WE SHALL DISCOVER BLISSFUL WELLSPRINGS OF UNITY
WITH AWARENESS OF THE SOURCE OF REAL SECURITY
WE UNITE
IN A CONTINUOUS
STATE OF KNOWING
OUR LOVING
AND LEARNING
AND CREATING
UNFOLDING
GRADUALLY JOINING ALL IN INNER HARMONY
IN THIS EVER-MOVING
EVOLVING
REALITY
WE ARE DEVELOPING OUR UNITY CONSCIOUSNESS
AS WE COME INTO
A UNIFIED STATE OF AWARENESS

FRACTAL TIME

IN THE ENERGETIC DANCE OF LIFE
WE ARE A PART
OF NATURES EVER CHANGING PATTERNS
WE WATCH THEM DART
IN THE QUANTUM OCEAN
OF THE CYCLIC UNIVERSE
WITH JOY
JOIN THE DANCE
IF NOT PERFECT YET
WE REHEARSE
THE PATTERNS MOVE TOO FAST
TO GET STUCK IN ANY FACT
ON YOUR LAPTOP SCREEN
LET FRACTALS
EXPAND
AND CONTRACT
SPATIAL PATTERNS
LIKE FIREFLIES
WE'RE ABLE TO FLASH
INTERLOCKING PATTERNS
WITH DASH SPLASH PASH AND PANACHE
SURMISE TIME DOING THE SAME
WITH AMPLIFICATION
FIND YOUR OWN HARMONY
WITH RHYTHM OF PULSATION
WHEN YOU CAN PSYCH AND DEVELOP
YOUR OWN SPACE/TIME CODES
MAKE YOUR OWN WAVES
NO OUTSIDE FORCES CAN MAKE INROADS
TURN YOUR OWN SPACE/TIME DIAL
AND ELIMINATE STATIC
AFTER ALL
YOU HAVE ALWAYS BEEN
ELECTROMAGNETIC

THE NEW DREAM

LET TWENTY THIRTEEN BEGIN THE NEW DREAM
OUR TRANSFORMATION TRULY BEGINNING
TIME TO GRADUATE FROM THIRD DIMENSION
WE HAVE COME THROUGH TRIALS BORING AND THRILLING
WE'VE SUFFERED WARS DISEASE STORM AND TENSION
WE'VE SURVIVED CHAOS AND DRAMAS GRIPPING
WE HAVE MASTERED CONFLICTING ENERGIES
NOW READY TO GRADUATE WITH HONOURS
AND TO EXPLORE OTHER REALITIES
WITHOUT INHIBITIONS STIGMAS AND DOGMAS

GAP YEAR

CAN WE FLOW
INTO KNOWING
ALL WE HOLD MOST DEAR
IF WE LIKE
TWENTY THIRTEEN
CAN BE OUR GAP YEAR
FOR THERE MAY BE A GAP
BETWEEN EXPECTATIONS
AND NEW REALITIES
HIGHER IMPLICATIONS
RELEASE ALL YOUR WORRIES
RELAX
TAKE IT EASY
NO JUDGMENT
NOTHING'S IMPOSSIBLE OR SLEAZY
BE
FIND YOUR PEACE
ENJOY
ALL OF YOUR FINER GIFTS
GRADUALLY
THROUGH OUR WORLD
THE HIGHER LIGHT SIFTS
YOU'RE READY TO ENJOY
YOU'RE READY TO EMPLOY
AND BASK IN LOVE-LIGHT
BESIDE POOL OF REMEMBRANCE
OF HUMANKIND'S DIVINITY
AND ASCENDANCE
INTO SUBTLE DIMENSIONS
WHEREIN
INTENTIONS
AFFIRMATIONS
AND TRUE VISUALIZATIONS
BECOME WHAT THEY SEEM
AS WE CREATE
THE
NEW
DREAM

MEDIA

HOW QUICK WE HUMAN BEINGS ARE
TO BLAME THE MEDIA
HOWEVER
TELEPATHY AND EMPATHY ARE QUICKER
LET'S FACE IT
OUR VOLATILE MINDS ARE OFTEN SNEAKIER
MIGHT WE FIRST
EXERT SOME MIND CONTROL WITHIN OUR OWN HEADS
SHALL WE RISE ABOVE THE VIOLENT
VENGEFUL AND SHALLOW
WHEN MEDIA KNOWS
THAT HUMANKIND'S ATTITUDES MELLOW
THEY WILL BE QUICKER THAN SLITHERY SNAKES
TO FOLLOW

RAISING FREQUENCY

HOW MANY WAYS ARE THERE TO RAISE OUR FREQUENCIES
WHAT WORDS GESTURES THOUGHTS
FEELINGS FOODS AND ENERGIES
DO WE TAKE ON
TO DETRIMENT
OR BETTERMENT
TO ADVANCED SOULS
OUR WHOLE BEING IS ELOQUENT
IS IT TIME TO DETACH FROM CROWD MENTALITY
IN ORDER TO CREATE LIGHTER REALITY
WHAT DO WE SEE AS OUR HIGHEST PRIORITIES
OUR NEGATIVITIES AND POSITIVITIES
APT TO SHOW IN THE WHOLE OF OUR LIFE'S EXPRESSION
POSTURE
HEALTH
COUNTENANCE
RELAXATION
AND TENSION
BEYOND DEMEANOUR
WHAT'S WRITTEN IN OUR AURA
WHAT DO WE EXPLORE IN OUR WHOLE WORLD'S AURORA
WHAT CAN OTHERS READ IN OUR DREAMS AND FANTASIES
IN THE VERY NATURE OF OUR CREATIVITIES

FIRMAMENT

METATRON KNOWS WE'RE READY TO BE INFORMED
OUR EARTH'S NEW FIRMAMENT IS NOW BEING FORMED
MANTLE OF PROTECTION AND TRANSFORMATION
BEAUTEOUS
IRIDESCENT
PRE-ASCENSION
BY 12-12-12 CRYSTALLINE GRID COMPLETED
FIRMAMENT REBIRTHED BY 12-21-12
AND FIRMLY ANCHORED AT THE MARCH EQUINOX
OF THE TRANSFORMING YEAR OF TWENTY THIRTEEN
DOES IT HAVE TO BE BELIEVED
BEFORE IT'S SEEN
TO BE COMPLETED BY TWENTY THIRTY EIGHT
WHEREVER YOU ARE BY THEN
YOU'LL NOT BE LATE
TWO ELLIPTICAL ARCHES
ONE CRYSTALLINE
BOTH HELPING EARTHLINGS TO EVOLVE AND REFINE
ONE WITH ELECTROMAGNETIC ENERGY
COLOUR PLATIMUM
ONE GOLDEN SYNERGY
ASSISTING ALL OF US
EVENTUALLY
INTO TWELFTH DIMENSION
FAR AS WE CAN SEE
BUT WE DO NOT HAVE TO TRY
NO WORRIES MATE
RELAX AND ENJOY
RISING
IN THE LOVELIGHT

December 2012 , the Sedona Journal of Emergence in the article on page 34

LONGEVITY

COME ON LOVE
IT IS NEVER TOO LATE TO BEGIN
HAVEN'T YOU NOTICED
LONGEVITY CREEPING IN
YOUR TIME CAN BE EXTENDED
IF YOU'RE HAVING FUN
DON'T LET ANYTHING END
BEFORE IT HAS BEGUN
ARE SOME OF YOUR TALENTS
HIDDEN UNDER BUSHELS
YOU WANTED TO COOK
DID THEY SAY
GO BLOW BUBBLES
WHAT
DID NOBODY
LET YOU DO
WHEN YOU WERE YOUNG
DO YOU HAVE PICTURES UNPAINTED
OR SONGS UNSUNG
IF YOU'VE A SENSE OF HUMOUR
TRY BEING A HAM
TO BE MUTTON DRESSED AS LAMB
MIGHT BE LOTS OF FUN

COSMIC SUNRISE

THIS IS A NEW COSMIC SUNRISE
LET ALL OLD WORRIES FADE AWAY
EXPECT SUPERLATIVE SURPRISE
SURPASS ALL YOUR EXPECTATIONS
NEW AWARENESS IS ON THE RISE

WITHER

IF THEY DON'T SEEM TO WANT TO GO AWAY
JUST PLANT YOUR OLD PROBLEMS IN PLASTIC POTS
FORGET TO MULCH
DON'T WATER ANY DAY
ALL WILL SOON CATCH ON
THEY ARE MISBEGOTS
LET THEM WITHER
BROWN FADES TO SEPIA
SEPIA GRADUALLY VANISHES
UNTIL MEMORY ITSELF LANGUISHES
YOU FORGET WHAT YOU WANTED TO FORGET
UNTIL WITHERED PROBLEMS HAVE POTS TO LET
YOU ASKED NO MORE QUESTIONS
TOLD NO MORE LIES
WITHERED PROBLEMS
WILL ATTRACT NO DEAD FLIES
IF YOU WONDER
THINK OF BUTTERFLIES

WHETHER

WHETHER THOU GOEST
IS UP TO YOU
WILL YOU JUMP
WHEN ANYONE SAYS BOO
YOU RUN YOUR OWN MIND
OR IT RUNS YOU
WAS IT OPEN
TO ALL WINDS THAT BLEW
YOU MAY SET IT NOW
TO BE ON COURSE
YOU KNOW THE WAY
TO ATTUNE TO SOURCE

YEAR OF MASTERY

TWENTY THIRTEEN
HAS BEEN CALLED
THE YEAR OF MASTERY
LIVE FROM YOUR HEART
AND THIS WILL NOT BE A MYSTERY
KNOW THAT YOU CAN BE
THE MASTER OF YOUR OWN JOURNEY
THINK FROM YOUR HEART
GIVE INTUITIVE BALANCE TO BRAIN
FEMININE QUALITIES EMERGE
AND BECOME INGRAIN
STAY ON YOUR OWN PATH
FROM WORRY AND JUDGMENT ABSTAIN
WHATEVER COMES
YOU KNOW YOU ARE ABLE TO DEAL WITH
AFFIRM THE BEST
EXPECT WONDERS
REWRITE YOUR OWN MYTH
HUMAN CREATIVITY REACHES FOR A NEW ZENITH

TREE OF LIFE

3 D EXPERIENCE
MEANT TO EXPRESS DUALITY
WE ARE BOUND TO BE PULLED TWO WAYS
WITH 3 D ENERGY
ARE YOU STILL IN FLUX
EXPERIENCING LIFE AT THE CRUX
WITH CONFLICT ON YOUR T V
AND CONFLICT IN YOUR OWN HOME
OR WHEREVER AND WHENEVER YOU MAY HAPPEN TO ROAM
WHAT IF IT'S ALL BEING GENERATED
IN YOUR OWN MIND
PROJECTED OUT IN ALL DIRECTIONS
CAUSING YOUR OWN BIND
HOW OFTEN DO YOU WISH
THAT YOU COULD LEAVE IT ALL BEHIND
STOP
CAN YOU HEAR ANCIENT ONES SPEAK
FROM FINER DIMENSION CALLING TO YOU
WITH LOVE PEACE HARMONY AND COMPASSION
SPEAKING THROUGH THE EONS
FROM PURE TRUTH AND FROM RIGHT ACTION
ARE YOU STILL IN 3 D BECAUSE YOU ARE CRAVING FRICTION
HAVE YOU AN ADDICTION TO DRAMA STRESS MISERY STRIFE
THE CHOICE IS YOURS
ALWAYS HERE WITH YOU IS THE TREE OF LIFE
MAJESTIC TREE
AMID HER BRANCHES
ALL POTENTIAL RIFE
DO YOU SEE ALL OF THE FEARFUL
DARKNESS WHIRLING BELOW
ENDLESS LIGHT SHINING FROM ABOVE
WAY UP IS ALL AGLOW
DO YOU KNOW YOU'VE ALWAYS BEEN FREE
ARE YOU WILLING TO CLIMB
UNTIL DOWN IS ALSO UP
YOU'RE ABLE TO FEEL SUBLIME
YOU KNOW ONENESS
EVERYTHING IS AT PEACE
WITH ALL YOU ARE
AND YOU KNOW THAT TERRA IS WHOLE
SHE IS HER OWN STAR

ADVENTURE

THIRD DIMENSION IS A VITAL EXPERIENCE
DON'T KNOCK IT
THIRD DIMENSION HAS TO BE A GRAND ADVENTURE
DON'T MOCK IT
WHEN READY TO CLOSE THAT DOOR
DON'T LET CRITICISM LOCK IT
IF YOU'RE STILL ENGROSSED
IN GRIPPING DRAMA ON THE OTHER SIDE
YOU'LL FEEL MORE THAN READY
WHEN REALITY BEGINS TO SLIDE
ODDITIES
MYSTICAL
AND UNEXPECTED
DO NOT ESCHEW
KNOWING THAT PARALLEL REALITIES CAN ALSO BE TRUE
WHEN TIME/SPACE IS RIGHT
OUTSIDE IS INSIDE
YOU KNOW YOUR OWN GUIDE
PROCEED IN SELF CONFIDENCE AND TRUST
AND BE IN YOUR OWN PRIDE
BUT YOU DON'T NEED
TO GIVE UTTERANCE TO YOUR SOLILOQUY
WHETHER YOU THINK IT HAS BEEN
EPIPHANY
OR EPITOME

DUALITY

IN DUALITY
WE EXPERIENCED
FROM THE RIDICULOUS TO THE SUBLIME
PERHAPS A WHOLE LOT MORE IN THE BETWEEN
ALL IN TECHNICOLOUR
AND ON WIDESCREEN
IN OUR SOULS
WE KNOW IT'S ALL BEEN SUPREME
AND WE SUSPECT IT'S ALWAYS BEEN A DREAM
SOMETIMES
POSSIBLY EVEN A BUMMER
OTHER TIMES YOU'RE A LONG DISTANCE RUNNER
DID YOU NEED A STRONGER SENSE OF HUMOUR
NOW THE SONG AND DANCE ARE NEARLY OVER
EXCEPT FOR CLAPPING
MUSIC
AND CREDITS
IS THERE SOMETHING THAT YOU WISH YOU COULD SAY
TO YOUR FELLOW ACTORS ALONG THE WAY

MARATHON

WE MIGHT AGREE
THAT 3 D HAS BEEN A MARATHON
SHOWING THAT
AT TIMES
ANYONE MIGHT BE RAPSCALLION
A TEST
ENDURANCE STRENGTH AND FIDELITY TO HONE
REQUIRING US TO GET CLEAR OUT OF OUR SAFETY ZONE
IF ONLY TO KNOW IT ENOUGH
TO FIND IT AGAIN
TO KNOW WE'RE NOT ALONE
HOWEVER FAR WE MAY ROAM
DID LAMBS NEED TO BE LOST
BEFORE THEY KNEW THE WAY HOME

DON'T TELL TALES

DO YOUR CRITICS IMPLY YOU ARE GOING OFF THE RAILS
SURELY YOU DO NOT BELIEVE OR REPEAT OLD WIVES' TALES
PROPAGANDA IS SIMPLY DESIGNED TO TAKE US IN
A HUMAN INVENTION
IS THE IDEA OF SIN
HONOURED MEMBER OF THE HUMAN RACE
YOU'VE ALWAYS BEEN
JUST WHAT YOU DO
IN THE PRIVACY OF YOUR OWN SPACE
IS YOUR BUSINESS
WHO SAID YOU MUST CONFORM OR CONFESS
OR EXCUSE OR EXPLAIN YOURSELF TO ANYONE ELSE
BUT DO MIND YOUR OWN DISPOSITION AND DEPORTMENT
DO HAVE THE GRACE NOT TO POLLUTE YOUR ENVIRONMENT
WITH YOUR GRUMPINESS OR SULLENNESS OR CRABBINESS
SO
FOR HEAVEN'S SAKE
DO WHATEVER YOU'D LOVE TO DO
TO RELIEVE YOUR OWN TENSION GRIEF
STRESS OR FRUSTRATION
IN AN IMPERFECT WORLD
TAKE CARE OF YOUR HAPPINESS
THUS TO ALL AROUND YOU
GREATER HAPPINESS IS SWIRLED
PERHAPS YOU MAY NEED TO RESORT
TO SOMETHING SUCH AS
DERVISH TURNING YOGA PUZZLES OR MEDITATION
COLD SHOWERS POW-WOW STEAM BATHS OR SELF TITILLATION
BY DRUMMING OR BELLY DANCING YOU CAN AVOID STRESS
CARD GAMES OF SOLITAIRE MINIATURE GOLF OR CHESS
ONCE YOU BEGIN TO TRULY ENJOY YOUR PLAY OR GAME
DEPRESSION AND ANXIETY CANNOT BE THE SAME
YOUR CRABBIEST DAYS WILL THANKFULLY BE BEHIND YOU
YOU WILL BE SO GLAD TO KNOW THAT
YOU DO WHAT YOU DO
DISREGARDING GOSSIP GAFFE CENSURE OR ACCOLADE
IT WILL NOT BE OFFENSIVE TO CALL A SPADE A SPADE
KNOWING THAT YOU ARE KEEPING
YOURSELF IN FINE FETTLE
UNLESS
YOU'RE STILL
A TEENSY WEENSY BIT
JUDGMENTAL

STORMY PETREL

HIGH STEPPER WITH PRIDE IS STORMY PETREL
TAKING ALL IN STRIDE
NEVER REGRETFUL
STORM GAIL FLOOD AND QUAKE
HELP EARTHLINGS AWAKE
CLEAR AWAY DEBRIS
ALLOW US TO SEE
PAST OUT OWN BLIND SPOTS
UNRAVEL OUR KNOTS
ELIMINATE WEED
GERMINATE NEW SEED
IF YOU EVER NEED WALK THROUGH ANY STORM
KNOW YOU'RE NOT ALONE
YOU ARE NEVER LORNE
KEEP LOVELIGHT EVER GLOWING IN YOUR HEART
REMEMBER YOUR OWN GRAND EXPANDING LIGHT
CAN ALWAYS PIERCE THROUGH
PENETRATE THE DARK
WE ON EARTH SEEMED LOST WHEN OUR FEAR WAS STARK
NOW LET DIVINE GRACE
EMBRACE
SET THE PACE
LIGHT FLOODING INNER
OUTER
HYPERSPACE

WHY

WHY DID WE CREATE
THE BUMPER CAR
THE ROLLER COASTER
FEATHER AND TAR
CHAMBERS OF HORRORS
NAMELESS TERRORS
PERHAPS WE CREATED ALL SUCH THINGS
IN ORDER TO SPLIT REALITY
AS A TEST OF OUR FIDELITY
SO THAT AT HEART WE CAN REMEMBER
ALL OF LIFE IS INTERCONNECTED
BY DIVINE GRACE IN ALL PURITY
ANYTHING AT ALL CAN BE MENDED
AND EVERYTHING IS RESTORABLE
EVERY LIVING THING TO BE TREASURED
EVERYONE AT TIMES ADORABLE
DID WE CHOOSE DISCOMBOBULATION
TO STIMULATE COMING SALVATION
WHATEVER HAPPENS
ALL WILL BE SAVED
IT IS TIME TO FORGIVE THE DEPRAVED
AND FORGET THAT THEY HAVE BEEN DEPRIVED
AND LET US FORGET THE WORD SORRY
WITH FORGIVENESS IF NECESSARY
SOME OF US ABLE TO LIFT OURSELVES
UP BY OUR OWN UNFASTENED BOOTSTRAPS
IF WE NEED HELP
HELP WILL ALWAYS COME
HELP MAY FALL DOWN FROM OUT OF THE CLOUDS
IT MAY FLY UP OUT OF THE MUDFLATS
HAVE NO FEAR
AS SOULS WE ARE ALL MATES
SOMEWHERE IN TIME
YOUR CHARIOT AWAITS

ATTUNE

IN THE THIRD DIMENSION
UPS AND DOWNS ARE RIFE
AND BEFORE WE KNOW IT
WE COULD BE IN STRIFE
SO ONE THING
THAT WE ARE FINALLY LEARNING
IS TO ATTUNE
FOR WHATEVER WE'RE DOING
WE CAN LIFT OURSELVES ABOVE STRIFE IN A TRIFE
AT THE SAME TIME
ENRICH THE QUALITY OF LIFE

ONE EARTH

OUR WORLD HAS LONG SEEMED TO BE
IN AN UNHOLY TANGLE
THE DAILY NEWS IS CHUCK FULL
OF DIRE SCANDAL AND WRANGLE
EXPERIENCING RESTLESS CONFLICT DISCORD AND SCHISM
THUS WE HAVE LONG EXPECTED AN ULTIMATE DIVISION
AT TIME OF THE 12 12 12 COMES THIS NEW REVELATION
WE COME TO THE OPENING
OF THE VISICA PISCIS
ENABLING US TO MELD
ALL IN THIS TRANSFORMATION
WE BIRTH OUR ELEVATION
INTO GRAND GROUP ASCENSION
ALL ON EARTH ARE BEING PROPELLED
INTO THE CRYSTALLINE
TO EXPERIENCE BLESSINGS OF HIGHER FIFTH DIMENSION
THERE WAS WIDE-SPREADING FEAR
BUT WE DID NOT DISINTEGRATE
SPURRED ON BY DIRE PREDICTION
WHOLE EARTH DID NOT SEPARATE
ONE UNITED EARTH WILL SAIL
THROUGH HER OWN OPEN STARGATE
NOT A SINGLE RENEGADE SOUL
WILL BE REQUIRED TO WAIT
EVERY PERSON WHO HAS COME
TO LIVE NOW ON MOTHER EARTH
ABLE TO BE SAVED
BAR NONE
EVEN THE SO-CALLED HOPELESS
LOST OR DEPRAVED
HAVE A PLACE UNDER TULA
CENTRAL SUN
PREPARED BEFORE OR AFTER DEATH
FOR THIS GRAND REDEMPTION
DIVINITY HAS GRANTED US COSMIC DISPENSATION
SIMPLY BECAUSE
EVERY SOUL HAS CHOSEN THIS SALVATION
BE GLAD
GET OUT OF YOUR BIND
LET ALL OF JUDGEMENT UNWIND
BECAUSE NOBODY AT ALL IS TO BE LEFT BEHIND

KINDNESS

IF YOU FEEL IT IS ABOUT TIME TO REST
IF THERE'S ONE SPECIAL THING TO REMEMBER
WITH WHICH QUALITY MIGHT HUMANS BE BLESSED
IF IT'S KINDNESS ITSELF
ALL WILL COME RIGHT
PLANET EARTH WILL FEEL SHE HAS BEEN STAR KISSED
WHEN ALL OF US
ARE KIND TO EACH OTHER
ALWAYS
FOREVER
WE'VE PASSED THE LOVE TEST

HAVE YOU BEEN KIND
TO A SNAKE TODAY
OR WHOEVER
CHANCED TO COME YOUR WAY

NO LONGER EARTHBOUND

WE'RE NO LONGER EARTHBOUND
WE ARE BIRDS ON THE WING
THERE ARE TIMES TO ALLOW
AS WE SIT BACK AND SING
AND THERE ARE TIMES
WHEN WE'D BETTER BEAR IT AND GRIN
BUT THERE ARE OTHER TIMES WHEN WE WILL NOT GIVE IN
THEN
WE KNOW IT IS TIME TO
DO
SOMETHING
BECAUSE WE LOVE TO

MEMORY LANE

BY THE BY
AND BY THE WAY
JUST ONE MORE LITTLE THING
HAVE YOU SEEN A SIGN
AT THE END OF MEMORY LANE
SUGGESTING
YOU MAY NO LONGER
WANT TO LINGER THERE
YOU COULD DANCE YOUR WAY OUT LIKE
GINGER AND FRED ASTAIRE
INSTEAD OF SITTING BACK IN YOUR TIRED ROCKING CHAIR
TO PROGRESS
MEMORIES MAY CAUSE SEVERE RESTRICTION
BECAUSE MEMORY LANE
IS UNDER RE-CONSTRUCTION

DIVINE ALCHEMY

SINCE TWENTY THIRTEEN IS TO BE OUR MAGIC YEAR
LET'S RECALL ALL THAT WE HAVE HELD TO BE MOST DEAR
FOR ALL PAST BLESSINGS LET'S UTTER A ROUSING CHEER
THEN
FOR A BLESSED FUTURE
BEYOND ALL BELIEF
LET US USE POSITIVE MAGIC FOR SWEET RELIEF
TO RISE ABOVE OLD CONCEPTS OF LIMITATION
STIMULATE OPTIMISM
ALLOW MUTATION
LET US LAUGH AND SING AND PLAY
LET US LOOP THE LOOP
AROUND ANY CORNER
WE MIGHT FIND A STARGATE
AS WE HUNT AND WE SWOOP
LET US DARE TO ELATE
COME ON GROUP
WE'RE READY
WE CAN ALL BE COCK-A-HOOP

(having written 5 last poems for this book
I think it's time for you to have your say
you may just want to have another look
decide whether you're feeling gay yea or neigh)

LAST WORD

May this book of poems be dedicated
to _The Sedona Journal of Emergence_
which has been my inspiration for many years

JEAN KATHARINE ROBERTS

Born in Boston in 1929, while my father was doing his doctorate at Harvard, Mother and I were sent back to the Idaho farm later in the year, after the depression hit, though we did return to Cambridge as soon as we could. When I was four we made our first real home on the edge of the desert in Tucson near the University of Arizona where Father began his teaching. I have been a wanderer ever since.

First an impoverished artist, then a dyslexic librarian, eventually a high school art teacher, I now teach Wholistic Art from the Spiritual Community of Findhorn in Scotland, (Art for Awareness and Personal Growth.) I usually teach small groups in my own home or in new age centres.

I have been a Theosophist and an eager student of the esoteric and occult especially since I belonged to a channelling group in Bondi Junction, N S W in the sixties. AQGWT4 was our contact.

In 1959 I finished my B A in Fine Arts at Mary Washington College of the University of Virginia, in 1960 I did my M S in Library Science at The University of Southern California and in 1989 I completed my M A in Arts and Consciousness at the John F. Kennedy University in Orinda, California. I spent about a year studying and working in the Findhorn Community in Scotland, and have spent many enlightening months in Sedona, Arizona.

I have live about half of my life in the U.S. of A. and half in Australia.

Last year I taught Transformative Art at Mystic Mountain in Corvallis, Oregon; this year I have been in a retreat mode, mainly for poetry writing. Now I am about to leave Woodend, Queensland for wherever I can find Transformative Art teaching.

kateartspeak@hotmail.com

Printed in the United States
By Bookmasters